Introducing Religions

Buddhism

Sue Penney

First published in Great Britain by Heinemann Library,
Halley Court, Jordan Hill, Oxford OX2 8EJ,
a division of Reed Educational & Professional Publishing Ltd

OXFORD FLORENCE PRAGUE MADRID ATHENS MELBOURNE
AUCKLAND KUALA LUMPUR SINGAPORE TOKYO IBADAN
NAIROBI KAMPALA JOHANNESBURG GABORONE
PORTSMOUTH NH (USA) CHICAGO MEXICO CITY SAO PAULO

First published 1997

ISBN 0 431 06643 4 hardback

01 00 99 98 97
10 9 8 7 6 5 4 3 2 1

ISBN 0 431 06650 7 paperback

01 00
10 9 8 7 6 5 4 3 2

British Library Cataloguing in Publication Data

Penney, Sue
  Buddhism. – (Introducing religions)
  1. Buddhism – Juvenile literature
  I. Title
  294.3

Designed and typeset by Artistix
Illustrated by Gecko Limited. Adapted into colour by Visual Image
Printed in Hong Kong

Acknowledgements

Thanks are due to C and J Erricker and Liz Powlay for reading and advising on the manuscript.

The publishers would like to thank the following for permission to reproduce photographs:

Andes Press Agency p. 42; Aspect Picture Library p. 37; Christophe Bluntzer/Impact Photos p. 20; The Bridgeman Art Library pp. 28, 29; The J Allan Cash Photo Library pp. 13, 22, 25, 33; Circa Photo Library pp. 19, 43; Bruce Coleman Ltd p. 6; Douglas Dickins pp. 10, 30; C M Dixon p. 23; Anil Goonewardene p. 27; Sally and Richard Greenhill p. 47; Robert Harding Picture Library pp. 31, 32, 35; Graham Harrison pp. 17, 18, 40; The Hutchison Library pp. 26, 46; Barry Lewis/Network p. 11; G Mermet/Impact Photos p. 44; Christine Osborne Pictures p. 45; Pana/Press Association p. 36; Ann and Bury Peerless pp. 8, 9, 38; Still Pictures p. 14; Topham Picturepoint p. 21; Zefa Pictures pp. 24, 34.

The publishers would like to thank Panos Pictures/Jean-Leo Dugast for permission to reproduce the cover photograph.

Every effort has been made to contact the copyright holders of any material reproduced in this book. Any omissions will be rectified in subsequent printings if notice is given to the publisher.

Contents

MAP: where the main religions began

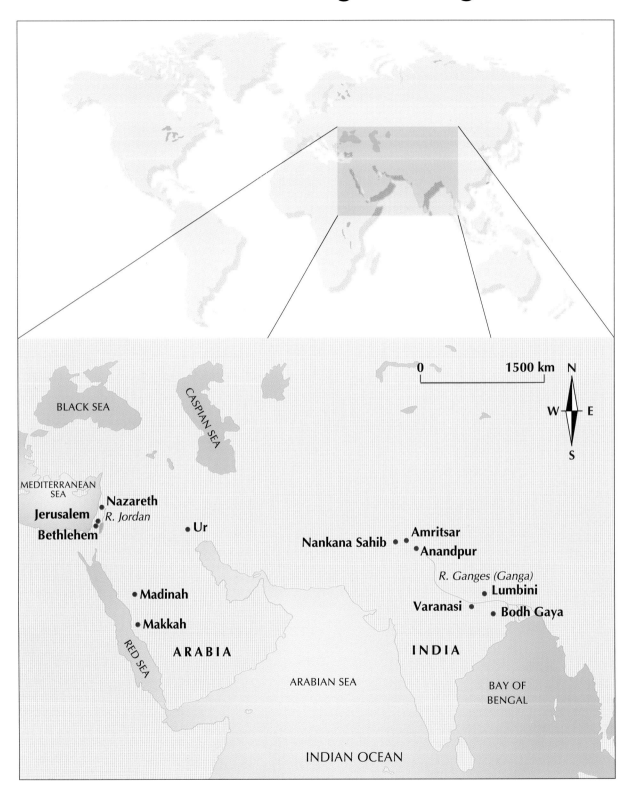

TIMECHART: *when the main religions began*

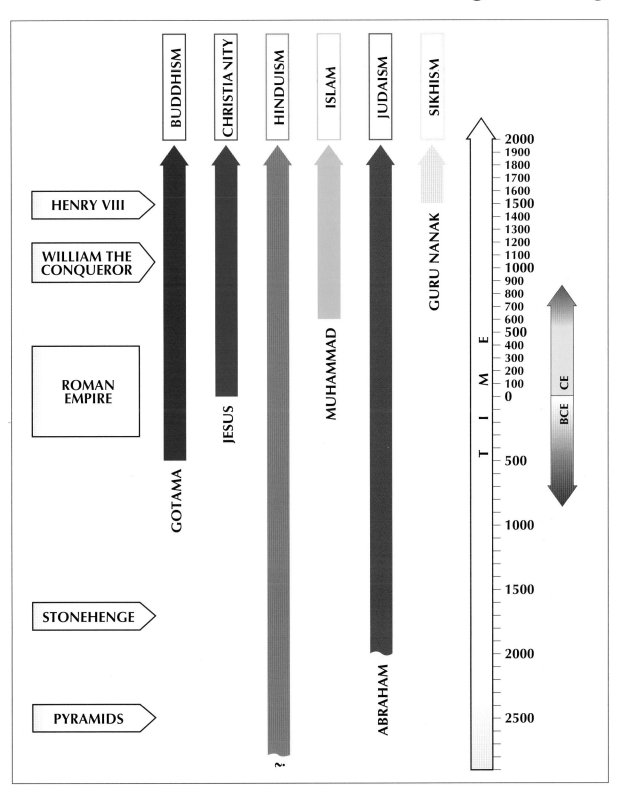

Note about dating systems   *In this book dates are not called BC and AD, which is the Christian dating system. The letters BCE and CE are used instead. BCE stands for 'Before the Common Era' and CE stands for 'Common Era'. BCE and CE can be used by people of all religions, Christians too. The year numbers are not changed.*

Introducing Buddhism

This section tells you something about who Buddhists are.

The teaching we call Buddhism began in India about 2500 years ago. Today, most Buddhists live in Asian countries like Thailand and Japan, but there are Buddhists in many countries.

What do Buddhists believe?

Buddhists follow the teachings of a man called Siddattha Gotama. He lived in India in the 6th century BCE. This man is called the **Buddha**. This was not his name. It is a special title. It means someone who has gained **Enlightenment**.

Enlightenment means being able to see things as they really are. (Think of turning on a light so you can see better.) Buddhists believe that the Buddha saw the truth about the world.

Buddhists do not believe that there is a God who is all-powerful. They do not believe that the Buddha was more than a man. He was important because he gained Enlightenment.

Rebirth

Buddhists believe that unless someone gains Enlightenment, when they die they will be born again.

A lotus flower

Buddhists believe that being born, growing old, dying and being reborn is a cycle which goes on and on. Breaking out of the cycle is called **Nirvana**. (See page 11.)

This is a sign for Buddhism.

New words
Buddha someone who has gained Enlightenment
Enlightenment understanding the truth about the way things are
meditation controlling your mind so that you can really concentrate
Nirvana the end of everything that is not perfect

Buddhists try to reach Nirvana by following the Buddha's teaching and by **meditation**. Meditation means training your mind so that you can really concentrate. (See page 22.)

Buddhist sign
The sign used most often for Buddhism is a wheel with eight spokes (like this one on the left).

The lotus flower

Buddhists often use the lotus flower to teach about how people should live. The lotus flower is a sign of things that are pure and good.

The lotus is a plant which belongs to the same family as the water lily. The plants grow at the bottom of the pond, in the mud. Then they rise to the top of the pond to flower. The flower is very beautiful. It does not show any sign of the mud in which it grows.

Buddhists say that this shows how people should rise above everything that is not right in their life, and gain Enlightenment.

The life of the Buddha

This section tells you about the life of Siddattha Gotama, the Buddha.

Siddattha's early life

Siddattha was an Indian prince. He was born in a place called **Lumbini**, in the country we now call Nepal. When he was born, wise men said that he would be great. But they said that if he ever saw anyone who was very unhappy, he would become the leader of a religion, not the leader of a country.

Siddattha's father wanted his son to be a great ruler. He ordered that no one who was sick or old should come near the palace. Siddattha was not to leave the palace grounds.

One day, when he was about 29, Siddattha disobeyed his father's orders. He went out riding.

While he was out, he saw an old man, and a sick man. He saw a funeral, with people weeping. He had never seen anything like this before. Then he saw a holy man who had given up everything he owned. He was trying to find the answers to the problem of suffering in the world. He was happy and content. Siddattha decided that he must try to find the answers to this problem, too.

Enlightenment

That night Siddattha left the palace and began his search for Enlightenment.

An old painting which shows Siddhatta leaving his palace

A temple near the bodhi tree

New words
bodhi tree the 'tree of wisdom'
  under which the Buddha gained
  Enlightenment
cremate to burn a body after
  death
Lumbini birthplace of the Buddha
stupas buildings where part of
  the Buddha's ashes were buried

He searched for six years.
One day, he sat down under
a tree to meditate. Today, this
tree is called the **bodhi tree**.
It means 'tree of wisdom'.

Siddattha meditated for a
day and a night, and there
he gained Enlightenment.
He understood why suffering
happens, and how it can be
stopped. From this time on,
he is called the Buddha.

The Buddha spent the rest of his
life teaching. He passed away at
the age of 80 (Buddhists do not
say he died). His body was
cremated, and the ashes were
buried in special buildings
called **stupas** (see page 25).

Siddattha's search for Enlightenment

Siddattha spent six years
searching for Enlightenment.
First he spent time learning from
two great teachers. They could
not teach him what he needed.

Then he spent many years with
five holy men. They ate and drank
almost nothing. The idea was
that if you force your body to
suffer, it becomes less important
to you. Siddattha found that
starving himself did not help him
to find answers to the questions
he was asking, so he began
eating again. It was after all this
searching that Siddattha began
to meditate under the bodhi tree.

The Three Jewels

This section tells you about some Buddhist teachings.

A jewel is something beautiful and precious. Buddhists say that these teachings are like jewels.

The First Jewel
The First Jewel is the Buddha. Buddhists respect him because he showed the way to Enlightenment.

Enlightenment is not the same as just knowing things. It means finding them out for yourself, and realizing they are true. (Think of learning to ride a bicycle. People can tell you what to do, but you still have to discover how to do it for yourself.)

Buddhists believe that only when they have gained Enlightenment can they stop being reborn and enter Nirvana.

The Second Jewel
The Second Jewel is the Buddha's teaching. This is called the **Dhamma**. This word means natural law. In other words, Buddhists believe that these teachings have always been there, and have always been true. They think the Buddha was important because he explained the laws so that people could understand them.

The Third Jewel
The Third Jewel is the **Sangha**. This word means everyone who follows the Buddha. It is used especially to describe Buddhist monks and nuns.

A Buddhist temple in Burma

Buddhists at
a monastery
in Scotland

Monks and nuns are men and women who have chosen to make their religion the most important thing in their lives.

Every day, Buddhists repeat these words:

*I take **refuge** in the Buddha*
I take refuge in the Dhamma
I take refuge in the Sangha.

This shows how important the three Jewels are.

New words

Dhamma 'natural law' – the Buddha's teachings
refuge somewhere you can go which is very safe
Sangha followers of the Buddha, especially monks and nuns

Nirvana

Buddhists say that it is not really possible to say what Nirvana is like. The word means going out, like a fire goes out because there is no wood or coal left. Nirvana is not life, and it is not death. 'You' no longer exist. There is a Buddhist story which shows how difficult it is to explain what Nirvana is like.

The story says that a fish and a turtle were friends. One day the fish asked the turtle to tell him what life was like outside the water. The turtle tried, but he had to give up. The fish could not understand, because he had no idea of the meaning of words like air and sky and grass. In the same way, it is impossible to explain Nirvana.

The Buddha's Teachinys (1)

This section tells you about the first part of the Buddha's teachings.

After his Enlightenment, the Buddha spent nearly 50 years teaching. Buddhists believe that the Buddha's teachings tell them how to live.

People usually divide the Buddha's teaching into three main parts. The first is the Three Signs of Being.

The Three Signs of Being

The Three Signs of Being are **dukkha**, **anicca** and **anatta**.

Dukkha – the First Sign

Dukkha means things that are not right. It means things like being in pain or really miserable. It also includes things like being bored and being uncomfortable. The Buddha said that dukkha is everywhere in life. No one can get away from it. His teaching was a way of rising above it.

Anicca – the Second Sign

Anicca is a way of saying that nothing lasts. Everything that we know is changing. This is easy to understand when you think about plants or animals or even people. Even things like mountains that seem to be there for ever do change slowly.

Anatta – the Third Sign

Anatta means no **soul**. Many religions teach that there is a soul or spirit which never dies. The Buddha said that there is no such thing. Buddhists believe in rebirth, but they do not believe there is a soul which goes on from one body to another.

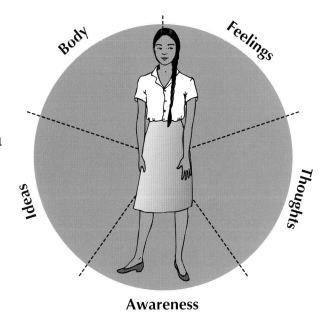

This diagram shows the Buddha's teaching about the five parts of a person.

Buddhists worshipping at a temple in Thailand

They believe that what carries on to the next life is **kamma**, the life-force a person makes in this life. Doing good things will lead to a higher life next time. Doing bad things will lead to a lower life next time. The only way to break out of this life-force is to reach Nirvana by following the Buddha's teachings and by meditating.

New words

anatta there is nothing called a soul
anicca nothing lasts
dukkha nothing is satisfactory
kamma life-force
soul a spirit which goes on living after a person's death

The five parts of a person

The Buddha taught that every person is made up of five parts. They have a body. They have feelings. They have ideas. They think. They have awareness – in other words, they can know about things that are going on around them. The Buddha said it is the way these five things are put together that makes each person different.

These five things change each time a person is reborn. So Buddhists do not think that there is a self or soul which makes a person what they are, and which carries on after they have died. They feel that it is the way that these five things come together in each person that makes that one person different from everyone else.

The Buddhu's Teachinys (2)

This section tells you about the Four Noble Truths.

The Four Noble Truths were the main part of the Buddha's first teaching which he gave after he had gained Enlightenment. He taught about the reasons why everything in the world is dukkha (not perfect).

He taught about what people can do to rise above it. He said that when people understood the Four Noble Truths, they could change their lives.

The First Noble Truth
Everything is dukkha, and dukkha is everywhere all the time.

The Buddha said that everything in the world is dukkha, because nothing can ever be exactly as we wish it to be. Every person's life includes the effect from the lives they have lived before. This is why no one's life can ever be perfect.

The Second Noble Truth
Dukkha is caused by being greedy and selfish.

Everybody thinks more about themselves than they do about others. We always want the best for ourselves. We prefer to do what we want rather than what other people want to do. (Think of when you are in the playground at break!) The Buddha said that being selfish is the cause of dukkha in the world.

Buddhists say that everything in life is dukkha.

14

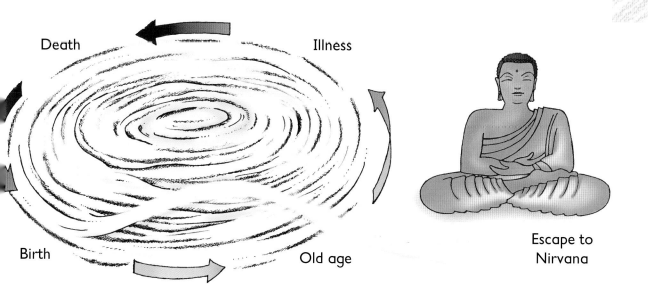

Death   Illness

Birth   Old age

Escape to
Nirvana

The circle of rebirth

The Third Noble Truth
Greed and selfishness can be stopped.

When you no longer want anything for yourself you can leave dukkha behind. This only happens when you have broken out of the circle of rebirth, and have reached Nirvana.

The Fourth Noble Truth
The way to stop selfishness is to follow the Noble Eightfold Path.

The Noble Eightfold Path is the way the Buddha taught that people should live. It is explained on pages 16–17.

The Buddha's teaching

When the Buddha gained Enlightenment, he could have chosen to leave earth at once and enter Nirvana. Instead, he chose to stay and teach other people the way to achieve Enlightenment, too.

His first teaching was to the five holy men who had been his friends before his Enlightenment (see pages 8–9). This teaching took place in the Deer Park just outside Varanasi, an important Indian city. He told the men first about the Four Noble Truths.

The Buddhu's Teachinys (3)

This section tells you about the Noble Eightfold Path.

The Buddha said that the way to Nirvana was the 'Middle Way'. He meant that you should not have too much or too little of anything. A life of luxury is no better than a life where you starve or punish yourself.

The path the Buddha taught about is called the Noble Eightfold Path. It shows eight ways that people should live. You need to follow all the ways. They all begin with the word right. Right means 'best possible', not just right or wrong.

Right understanding
This means looking at life in the right way and accepting that the Buddha's teaching is true.

Right thought
Your mind has a lot of power, so it must be used in the right way. Thinking about other people in the right way will mean that you are not selfish.

Right speech
You should make sure that your words are always kind and helpful. Right speech also means not telling lies or swearing.

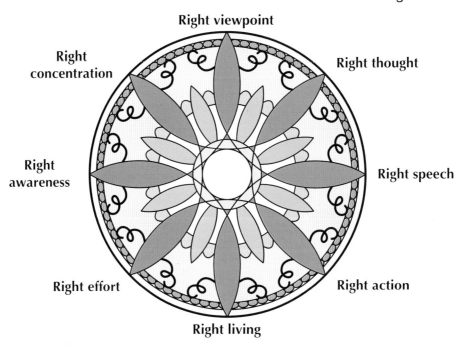

The Noble Eightfold Path

Candles are important in Buddhist worship.

Right living
You should not have a job which harms others, or means you need to kill things.

Right effort
A Buddhist must work hard to do good things, as well as avoiding bad things.

Right awareness
You need to train your mind so that you see things around you in the right way.

Right action
You should not kill or steal, and you should treat other people well. You should not do anything which harms your body, like smoking.

Right concentration
You can train your mind to concentrate by meditation. This helps you to be a calm and peaceful person.

'The best of paths'

There is a famous Buddhist teaching called the Dhammapada. In this teaching, the Buddha said that the Noble Eightfold Path was the best of paths. But he gave this warning:

'It is you who must make the effort'.

In another teaching, the Buddha described how most people lived.

He said that they were like people who were struggling to walk across ground which was very muddy. They could only be helped out of the mud by people who were standing on firm ground.

The Noble Eightfold Path, said the Buddha, is the way to find this firm ground.

The two main groups of

This section tells you about the two main groups of Buddhists today.

There are millions of Buddhists in the world, and they all follow the teachings of the Buddha. Of course, not all of them think in exactly the same way about the teachings. This means that there are different groups. The groups are called 'schools'.

In Buddhism, there are two main schools.

Theravada Buddhists
Theravada means 'teachings of the elders'. An elder is a leader of a religion who is respected.

Theravada Buddhism teaches that every person must gain Enlightenment for themselves. The Buddha showed people the way in his teachings. Buddhists follow him as a guide. Theravada Buddhists do not pray to the Buddha.

Many Theravada Buddhists think that the best way to live is as a monk or a nun. They can concentrate on their religious life, because they do not have to think about a job, a family or running a home.

Mahayana Buddhism
Mahayana means 'great vehicle'. This is a way of saying that there is room for different ways of reaching Nirvana.

Mahayana Buddhists follow the same basic teachings as Theravada Buddhists. Mahayana Buddhism sometimes explains the ideas in a different way from Theravada Buddhism.

Theravada Buddhist monks in Burma

Buddhists

Mahayana Buddhists think that there have been many Buddhas and other people called **Bodhisattvas**, who can help them in their lives. Mahayana Buddhists pray to them for help, and meditate to become more like them.

A statue of a Bodhisattva

New words

Bodhisattva person who has gained Enlightenment but who has chosen to be reborn to be able to help others
Mahayana 'great vehicle'
Theravada 'teachings of the elders'

Bodhisattvas

Bodhisattvas are found in the teachings of Mahayana Buddhism. They are men and women who have gained Enlightenment, so they could enter Nirvana. Instead, they choose to be reborn, so that they can help other people to gain Enlightenment, too.

Bodhisattvas are filled with peace and joy because of the way they have trained their minds. There are many thousands of Bodhisattvas. Mahayana Buddhists pray to them for help in achieving Enlightenment, and for help in their daily lives, too.

Mahayana teaching says that any good Buddhist could become a Bodhisattva in the future.

Other Buddhist groups

This section tells you about three branches of Mahayana Buddhism.

Zen Buddhism

Zen is a Japanese word which means meditation. Zen Buddhists say that meditation is very important. They meditate for many hours each day. They say that Enlightenment comes as a flash of understanding.

Zen Buddhists aim to silence thoughts which are unhelpful. They call this 'training the mind'. At last, this will lead to Enlightenment. Zen Buddhist monks often live very strictly.

Pure Land Buddhism

Pure Land Buddhists pray to the Buddha Amida, who is Lord of the Pure Land.

After life in this world, the Pure Land is a place without suffering where it is easier to achieve Nirvana. Pure Land Buddhists believe that Amida will help them to get there. They use a special prayer to Amida. It is 'Nembutsu Amida', which means 'I call on you, Amida'. Prayers which are repeated over and over again like this are called **mantras**. Buddhists believe that mantras have special power.

A Zen Buddhist monastery

Tibetan Buddhism

Tibetan Buddhists believe that a monk called the Dalai Lama is special. They believe he is an appearance of the Bodhisattva who is most special for the country of Tibet.

Mantras and prayers to this Bodhisattva are written on prayer wheels and flags. As the wheels turn and the flags blow in the wind, Tibetan Buddhists believe that the prayers are repeated over and over again. Making prayers which are repeated like this is a way of getting **merit**. Merit is a reward for doing good things. It helps you on your way to Nirvana.

New words

mantra prayer which Buddhists believe has special power
merit reward for doing good things in life

Prayer wheels

A prayer wheel is a tube of metal or wood which has the prayer carved on the outside, or written on paper and rolled up inside it. The wheel is fixed in place by a rod through the middle.

Tibetan Buddhist temples have prayer wheels. Some are bigger than a person, and need two or three people pushing together to turn them.

Other prayer wheels can be held in the hand. They can be turned because they have a small weight to make the prayer drum at the top turn, while the handle stays still. The faster the prayer wheel turns, the more prayers are repeated, and so the more merit is earned.

Prayer wheels and prayer flags at a temple in Nepal

Worship

This section tells you about how Buddhists worship.

Some Buddhists do not like using the word worship, because it usually means praying to God or gods. Worship in this book means the way Buddhists meditate and read the **scriptures**.

There is no special day of the week when Buddhists worship. Days before the moon is new, full or at half-moon are important. Full moon days are most important of all, because the Buddha is said to have been born, Enlightened and passed away at this time.

This woman is meditating.

Meditation
Most Buddhists think that meditation is the most important part of worship. Meditation means controlling your mind so that you can concentrate on things that are really important. Buddhists believe that meditating will help them to achieve Nirvana.

Worship on your own
Buddhists who are worshipping on their own usually meditate.

They also read from the scriptures. Buddhists may burn incense, which is a sweet-smelling perfume. They may offer small presents to an image (statue) of the Buddha.

Worship usually includes lighting candles. Buddhists believe that their light is a way of showing that the Buddha's teaching helps you to see important things.

Mahayana Buddhists pray to Bodhisattvas as part of their worship.

Worship in a group

Buddhists usually meet for worship in a special building called a temple. There is usually a room which contains a **shrine**. This is beautifully decorated with gold. It contains an image of the Buddha. There are no seats in a shrine room. Worshippers sit on the floor. They bow or put their hands together. Sometimes they lie flat on the floor. These are ways of showing how much they respect the image. People offer gifts of flowers and incense.

Offering gifts to the image

New words

scriptures books containing important teachings and stories
shrine special place for worship

The Five Precepts

A precept is a guide or rule for how you should live.

Buddhists think there are five precepts which are most important. They are the guides for living your life as a Buddhist, so all Buddhists are expected to follow them.

These five precepts are:

- *not to harm anything which is alive;*
- *not to take anything which has not been given;*
- *not to have affairs;*
- *not to talk carelessly or unkindly;*
- *not to drink alcohol or use drugs wrongly.*

Buddhists try to keep these five rules very carefully in their lives.

Where Buddhists worship

This section tells you about the different places where Buddhists worship.

Buddhists usually worship in front of shrines, either in a temple or at home.

Shrines

A shrine is a place which is special to people who follow a particular religion. A Buddhist shrine contains an image of the Buddha. It usually contains holders for flowers and candles, too. Many shrines are beautifully decorated.

Monasteries

In countries where most people are Buddhist, there are many monasteries. Ordinary people often go there to worship and study. Many children go to the local monastery to be taught to read and write by the monks.

Many monasteries are like a small village, with lots of buildings and huts where the monks live (see pages 40–1). The most important room in a monastery is the shrine room. This is used for worship, and also for meetings of the monks.

Stupas

Many Buddhists go to worship at important stupas. A stupa is a sort of building which is shaped like a rounded hill. After the Buddha had passed away, his body was cremated, and the ashes were taken to eight different places which had been important in his life.

A Japanese Buddhist woman worshipping at a shrine in her home

This stupa is at Bodnath in Nepal. The eyes are to show that the Buddha sees everything.

Stupas were built where the ashes were buried. Another two were built, one over the place where his body had been burned, and one where the container which had held the ashes was buried.

This made ten stupas which contain remains of the Buddha.

Later, other stupas were built to remember Buddhists who were special because they were teachers or holy people.

Monastery gardens

The garden is an important part of a Buddhist monastery. It often contains trees which give shade from the sun. This helps to make the monastery calm and peaceful.

The Buddha taught that nothing lasts. Plants show that this is true.

They grow and die, then their seeds grow again. In Zen Buddhist monasteries, gardens often include rocks and stones. These are set out carefully and the stones are raked (look at the picture on page 20). This helps to make the garden a restful place to meditate.

Buddhist scriptures

This section tells you about the Buddhist scriptures.

After the Buddha

When the Buddha was teaching, everyone remembered what he said. Many people in those days could not read or write, and even important things were not often written down.

For about 400 years after the Buddha passed away, all the teaching was passed down by Buddhist monks. There were meetings to check that everything was still being remembered correctly. Then people began to think that it should be written down.

Reading the scriptures

There are two main collections of teaching. A collection of teaching is called a **canon**. The two canons have the names of the languages in which they were first written. The **Pali** Canon is used by Theravada Buddhists. The **Sanskrit** Canon is used by Mahayana Buddhists. The Pali Canon was written down first. It is also called the **Tipitaka**.

The Tipitaka

Tipitaka means 'three baskets'. It is probably called this because it was first written on palm leaves which were kept in baskets.

The first basket contains the rules which monks should follow, and some stories. The second basket contains the teachings of the Buddha. The third basket contains writings which help to explain the Buddha's teachings.

The most important basket is the second one. It is called the **Sutta** Pitaka. A sutta is a small piece of teaching. The most important part is the Path of Teaching. It contains the Four Noble Truths and the Noble Eightfold Path.

Buddhist nuns in Britain studying the scriptures

Mahayana Buddhist scriptures

Mahayana Buddhists believe that two of the most important teachings are the Diamond Sutra and the Lotus Sutra. There are also 'extra' teachings of the Buddha in the Sanskrit Canon, which are not included in the Pali Canon.

New words

canon collection of scriptures
Pali old language, said to have been spoken by the Buddha
Sanskrit very old Indian language
sutta (Sanskrit sutra) a small part of the teaching
Tipitaka Buddhist teachings

Pali and Sanskrit

Pali and Sanskrit are two very old languages. The Buddhist scriptures were written down in both these languages. The fact that they were written in two languages is the reason why many Buddhist words can be spelt in two ways.

For example, Siddattha Gotama can be spelt Siddhartha Gautama. The first is the Pali spelling, the second is the Sanskrit. In the same way, sutta can also be spelt sutra, dhamma can also be spelt dharma. It does not really matter which spelling you use, because neither is better than the other. They are both just as correct, but you should not swap between the two.

Symbols in Buddhism

This section tells you about some of the symbols which Buddhists use.

A symbol is a way of showing something without using words. Using a symbol means that complicated things can be made clear without needing a long explanation. Buddhism uses many different symbols.

Flowers

The lotus flower is often used as a symbol for Buddhism. This was explained on page 7. Flowers are often used as a symbol of the Buddhist belief that everything is dukkha, too. They are pretty, but they soon die. They show that everything in life is not perfect.

Candles

Candles are used as a symbol of the Buddha's teaching. Just as a candle brings light to a dark room, so Buddhists believe that what the Buddha taught can show them the way to live. Candles are often used in worship.

Images of the Buddha

Images of the Buddha include lots of symbols which show that he was a special person. For example, the Buddha is often shown with a 'dome' on the top of his head. This shows that he had special talents. He is often shown with a mark on his forehead, called the third eye. This shows he could see things ordinary people cannot see.

An image of the Buddha (notice the special symbols)

A mandala

They also show that he could hear things that other people could not hear.

Mandalas

Mandalas are especially important in Tibetan Buddhism. They are complicated patterns usually made with coloured sand. Mandala means 'circle', and they are made up of circles, triangles, squares and diamonds. Sometimes mandalas include pictures of the Buddha or a Bodhisattva as well. Many Buddhists use mandalas to help them meditate.

He is shown with knotted hair, which is a sign that he was a very holy man. His long ears show that he came from an important family.

New word
mandala special pattern

The wheel of life

The wheel of life is a special sort of mandala which shows the Buddha's teaching. It has several pictures arranged in rings in a circle. The largest circle is the rim. It shows the twelve stages humans go through between birth and death. Inside this are possible places where people can be reborn.

In the centre is the hub with three animals. They show things that can go wrong in people's lives. The snake is a symbol of hatred. The cockerel is a symbol of greed. The pig is a symbol of ignorance. These things keep the wheel of life turning. The Buddha's teaching was about getting rid of them.

Pilgrimage

This section tells you about some of the important places where Buddhists go on pilgrimage.

A **pilgrimage** is a special journey people make because of their religion. Buddhists may go to places where the Buddha lived or taught. They believe this will help them in their own search for Enlightenment.

Lumbini

The Buddha was born at a place called Lumbini. This is now in the country called Nepal.

A community of monks live there and there are temples where people can meditate. There is a stone which says on it 'Here the Buddha was born'.

Bodh Gaya

Bodh Gaya is the place in India where the Buddha gained Enlightenment. Buddhists go there from all over the world, and it is one of the most important places of pilgrimage. A bodhi tree grows there. It is said to have grown from a seed of the tree that the Buddha sat under when he was meditating.

The Shwe Dagon temple in Burma

*Sunrise at
Sri Pada*

Stupas

Many Buddhists visit the stupas where part of the Buddha's ashes were buried. When they visit a stupa, Buddhists walk around it three times. This remembers the Three Jewels, which are the most important part of Buddhist teaching.

Sri Pada

Sri Pada is a mountain in Sri Lanka. It is very important for Buddhists because they believe that the Buddha visited it. At the top is a stone which has marks like footprints on it. Buddhists believe that these were made by the Buddha.

New word

pilgrimage journey made because of your religion

Buddhists and the moon

The moon is important for Buddhists. The Buddhist year follows the changes in the moon rather than the sun, and all Buddhist festivals take place at the time of the full moon.

Buddhists believe that the Buddha was born, achieved Enlightenment and passed away at the time when the moon was full.

The most important days of the month for Buddhists are the days before the moon is full or is new. On these days, many Buddhists make a special effort to go to the temple or a monastery and meditate.

Festivals in Thailand

This section tells you about festivals in Thailand, a Theravada Buddhist country.

Songkran

Songkran takes place in April and lasts for three days. It includes the Thai New Year.

People go to the monasteries, and give presents like food and flowers to the monks. New Year is a new start, so everyone wears new or clean clothes.

Water is very important in the festival of Songkran. There are boat races and water fights.

The festival ends when the bells in monasteries and temples are rung three times. This happens at midnight on the third day.

Wesak

The festival of Wesak gets its name from the month in which it is celebrated. The festival remembers the Buddha's birth, his Enlightenment and his passing away. Theravada Buddhists believe that these three things all happened on the day when the moon was full in the month of Wesak (May or June in the Western calendar). Wesak is one of the most important Buddhist festivals.

Water fights are part of the celebrations at Songkran.

In Thailand, the people visit the monasteries at Wesak. A special part of the celebration includes pouring perfumed water over the image of the Buddha in the shrine. At night, the image is taken out of the shrine and put on a platform outside. The people walk around it carrying lamps. This means that the image is surrounded by light. It reminds people of the 'light' of the Buddha's teaching.

Pouring perfumed water over the image of the Buddha

Kathina

Kathina takes place at the end of the rainy season in Thailand. People take presents to the monasteries as a way of saying thank you to the monks for all the work they do during the year. The monks are not allowed to own anything themselves, so the presents are given to the monastery.

Being kind to all creatures

The Buddha taught that it was important to be kind to everything that is alive. Buddhists follow this teaching at the festival of Songkran.

The festival happens at the time of year when there is no rain in Thailand, so many of the small rivers dry up. Sometimes fish are trapped in the ponds that form as the rivers stop running. The people collect these fish, and keep them in deeper water until Songkran. Then they let them go into the deep rivers. Sometimes they let go birds which have been kept in cages. Buddhists believe that as well as being kind to the animals, they are earning merit for themselves, too.

Festivals in Sri Lanka

This section tells you about festivals in Sri Lanka, which is also a Theravada Buddhist country.

Wesak

Wesak is the most important Buddhist festival in Sri Lanka. It remembers the Buddha's birth, his Enlightenment and his passing away. People light their houses with lamps and there are plays and dancing to celebrate the festival. Everyone remembers the Buddha's teaching about kindness and makes a special effort to be kind to others.

Poson

Poson is a special festival for Sri Lanka. It remembers the time when Buddhism was brought to Sri Lanka from India. The two **missionaries** who came to tell the people about Buddhism arrived in the town of Mihintale. Today, special plays are put on in this town, to remind people of how important the monk and the nun were.

Esala Perahera

Esala Perahera takes place in the month of August. The festival is held in the town of Kandy, and lasts for ten days.

The procession at Esala Perahera

Dancing is part of many festivals.

A temple in Kandy was built to keep something Buddhists think is very precious. It is one of the Buddha's teeth, kept in a special container. Every year there is a procession through the town. Over a hundred elephants take part. The most important elephant carries a container which is an exact copy of the real one. That is far too precious to be allowed on the streets. Esala Perahera is also a time for fun. There are fairs and dancers to entertain people watching the procession.

New word

missionary a person who travels to another country to tell people about their beliefs

Buddhism comes to Sri Lanka

In about 250 BCE, the king of Sri Lanka decided he wanted to know more about the teachings of the Buddha. He sent a message to the ruler of India, who was a Buddhist called Asoka.

Asoka sent his son Mahinda to Sri Lanka to tell the king about Buddhism. The king listened to what Mahinda said, and became a Buddhist. Then Asoka sent his daughter, who was a Buddhist nun. She took with her a branch of the bodhi tree from Bodh Gaya. This was planted near the town of Mihintale. This tree is still alive, and people think it is the oldest tree in the world.

35

Festivals in Japan

This section tells you about Buddhist festivals in Japan, which is a Mahayana Buddhist country.

New Year

For Japanese Buddhists, the day before New Year is one of the most important days of the year. This is when the Evening Bells ceremony takes place. At midnight, the bells in every Buddhist temple in Japan are rung 108 times. Japanese Buddhists think about ways in which they can live better lives in the year to come.

Obon

Obon is the most important Buddhist festival in Japan. It takes place in July. It is a time when Buddhists remember people in their family who have died. They believe that the spirits of people who have died come back to the family home for the three days of the festival. They light lamps to show them the way, and put flowers on the family shrine. Mahayana Buddhists believe that the Buddha can help you in your life, so praying to the Buddha is part of this festival.

One of the stories which Japanese Buddhists remember at Obon is about how the Buddha helped the mother of one of his friends. She was in the land of ghosts, and the Buddha pulled her out.

Ringing the bell at a temple in Japan

*Looking after graves
is part of Higan*

Some stories say that he pulled her out with a rope, so tug-of-war contests are often held.

Higan

Higan takes place twice a year, on the days when day and night are the same length. It is a time for remembering friends and relatives who have died.

Buddhists go to **cemeteries** to clean and look after their graves. They decorate them with flowers. They offer prayers for the people who have died.

New word

cemetery place where dead bodies are buried

Why are the bells rung 108 times?

At the Evening Bells ceremony, the bells are rung 108 times. This is a special number for Buddhists. There are several reasons for this.

The most important reason is because Buddhist teaching says that 108 is the number of things that go wrong in people's lives.

This includes things like greed and laziness. Buddhists believe that every ring of the bells helps them to get rid of one of these faults. Listening to the bells also gives Buddhists a chance to think about the things that are wrong with their lives, and promise that they will do better in the year that is coming.

The history of Buddhism

This section tells you a little about the history of Buddhism.

Early days

Buddhists believe that there have been other Buddhas, and there will be Buddhas in the future. Siddattha Gotama was the Buddha who began the Buddhist teaching for the time that we live in.

When he began teaching after his Enlightenment, a group of people became his followers. They included the Buddha's own son, Rahula. For 45 years, the Buddha travelled all over India and nearby countries, teaching people about the best way to live.

Emperor Asoka

After the Buddha had passed away, the people who had known him carried on his teaching. More and more people became interested in Buddhism.

One of the people who heard about it was the **Emperor** of India who was called Asoka. He ruled almost the whole of what we call India from 273 BCE to 232 BCE.

Asoka had fought many battles. He was worried about the suffering he had caused. He became a Buddhist, and tried to rule the country by following the teachings of the Buddha.

Asoka helped people to learn more about Buddhism. He ordered pillars to be built in places where important things had happened to the Buddha.

A pillar from the time of Asoka

This map shows where most Buddhists live today.

This map shows where most Buddhists live today.

These pillars were of stone and had writing carved on them explaining why they were there.

The spread of Buddhism

As Buddhism spread from one country to another, people did not always think that the same teachings were important. Some people began to think more about one teaching than another. This is why today there are different groups. They all follow the teachings of the Buddha, but they do not all follow them in the same way.

Buddhism today

Today there are two main groups of Buddhists. These groups are called Theravada Buddhists and Mahayana Buddhists. Most Buddhists live in the Far East.

Buddhism is the main religion in Bhutan, Burma, Cambodia, Japan, Laos, Sri Lanka, Thailand and Vietnam. It is also important in other countries like India and China. Buddhist customs, especially festivals, are often very different in different countries.

Many Buddhists do not go to temples, but worship at their shrines at home. This makes it difficult to know how many Buddhists there are in the world today. Most people think that there are at least 350 million. Some people think that there may be as many as 600 million.

Monks and nuns

This section tells you about the way Buddhist monks and nuns live.

Buddhist monks and nuns are men and women who spend their lives meditating and reading the scriptures. Nuns and monks live in the same way, but there are many more monks than nuns, so this section is about monks.

Who can become a monk?
Any Buddhist man can become a monk. Buddhists do not expect a monk to stay in a monastery all his life. Especially in Theravada Buddhist countries, boys often become monks for just a few years.

Being in the monastery is like being at school. When the boys grow up, they leave and find other jobs. Many adults join the monastery for a few months or years, so that they can learn more about Buddhism before going back to their normal lives.

Where do monks live?
Monks live in a monastery. Sometimes they have their own room. Often they live in huts in forests in the grounds of the monastery. The furniture is very simple – a table or stool, and a mat to sleep on. Especially in Zen Buddhism, all the monks may sleep in one big hall. Monks do not own anything except the robes they wear.

A Thai Buddhist monk studying outside his hut

They also have necessary things like a bowl for food and a razor to shave their head. Anything else – books for example, or pens and paper – belongs to the monastery, not the monk.

What do monks do?

Monks often spend most of the day on their own, reading and meditating. Sometimes they read and meditate in groups.

Many monks work as teachers or help people in some other way. They also do necessary jobs in the monastery.

Monks often eat only one meal a day, always before midday. After this they **fast** until the next day, although they are allowed to drink water.

Where do monks get food?

Monks are given their food and everything they need by people who live near the monastery. Sometimes people give money instead. This is called giving **alms**. It is not begging, because giving to the monks is part of a Buddhist's duty. It helps the person to earn merit.

New words

alms giving food and things that are needed

fast go without food and drink for religious reasons

Precepts for monks and nuns

There are five precepts which all Buddhists try hard to keep in their lives. These were described on page 23. Nuns and monks keep the five precepts very carefully. There are also another five precepts, which all monks and nuns are expected to keep. Some other Buddhists choose to keep them, too. These precepts are:

- *not to eat after midday;*
- *not to go anywhere where there is music or dancing;*
- *not to use perfume or jewellery;*
- *not to sleep on a soft bed;*
- *not to accept gifts of money.*

Keeping these rules helps nuns and monks to live simply so that they can concentrate on their worship.

Buddhism in the West

This section tells you about Buddhism in Western countries.

Until about a hundred years ago, Buddhism was not known in Western countries. The only Buddhists were in the countries where Buddhists had lived for hundreds of years.

The first Buddhist missionary to teach in Britain arrived in 1893. Since then more people have been able to move to other countries. Where Buddhists have done this, they have taken their Buddhism with them. In the last hundred years, too, travel has become much easier.

People are more used to going to other countries, and learning about life there. Some people have become interested in the Buddha's teachings, and have become Buddhists themselves.

Western Buddhist monasteries

Most Buddhists in Western countries work at ordinary jobs. Most do not become monks or nuns, but there are some Buddhist monasteries. Monks and nuns live in the same way as monks and nuns in countries where most people are Buddhist. They live very simply, and meditate and teach.

A Buddhist temple in London

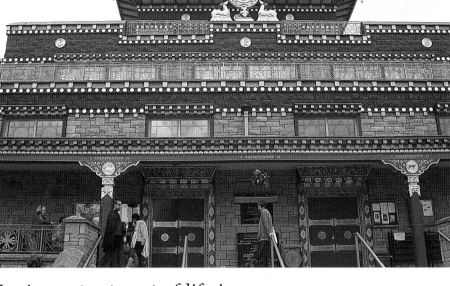

A Tibetan Buddhist monastery in Scotland

An important part of life in a Western monastery is arranging **retreats**. A retreat is a special time when people can leave their normal lives. They go to the monastery and live like a monk or nun for a few days or weeks. This gives people the chance to be with other Buddhists. They can also spend more time meditating and reading the scriptures.

In 1991, there were about 130,000 Buddhists living in Britain and about 140,000 in Australia. The largest number of Buddhists follow the teachings of Theravada Buddhism.

New word
retreat special time away from ordinary life

Friends of the Western Buddhist Order

The Friends of the Western Buddhist Order is one of the most important groups of Buddhists in Western countries. Their monks do not live in monasteries or wear robes. They run centres where other Buddhists and people who are interested in Buddhism can come to worship. They have centres in Britain and Europe as well as in America and Australia.

The teaching of this group uses the most important parts of the Buddha's teaching, but they also believe it is important for Buddhism to fit with the way people live today.

Special occasions (1)

This section tells you about important things which happen to young Buddhists in Burma and Thailand.

In countries like Burma and Thailand, older relatives prepare gifts for a new baby. A cradle is made ready, with clothes in it. When the baby is put in the cradle for the first time, the gifts are placed around it. The gifts are small useful things like books or tools which the child will need later in life.

Shaving the baby's head

The main **ceremonies** for a baby happen when it is a month old.

First, the head is shaved. This goes back to the Buddha's teaching about life-forces which carry on from one life to the next. The hair is a sign of a bad life-force from a previous life, so Buddhists get rid of it.

Then special cotton is tied around the baby's wrists, which the parents hope will bring it luck. The baby is often given its name, too. Sometimes monks suggest the name. Food is always given to the monks when a baby is born.

Joining a monastery

Many Buddhist boys join a monastery for a short time.

A school for Buddhist monks in Thailand

Many Buddhist boys are taught by monks.

In Burma and Thailand, almost all boys join a monastery when they are about ten years old.

The special ceremony when a boy joins the monastery is called **ordination**. In Burma, the boy acts out the story of Siddhatta Gotama leaving his palace and becoming a monk.

His head is shaved, like the other monks. He is also dressed in the special monk's robes.

New words

ceremony celebration of a special event

ordination ceremony in which a person becomes a monk or nun

Ceremonies in different countries

Buddhism teaches that the way you live is far more important than anything else. This is because of the Buddhist teachings about birth and rebirth. For Buddhists, birth and death are only stages on the way to another life. This means that there is no fixed teaching about the way ceremonies should be held.

People who live in different countries often celebrate occasions like birth or death in different ways.

Most Buddhists follow the way that things have always been done in their country. This means that the customs for birth or death may be quite different in different countries.

Special occasions (2)

This section tells you about the Buddhist ceremonies for marriage and death.

Marriage

In most countries where Buddhists live, the parents of a young man or woman suggest a person for them to marry. When a couple have agreed to marry, astrologers suggest a good date for the wedding. Astrologers are people who tell your future by studying the stars.

The marriage ceremony usually takes place in the bride's home. A male relative of the bride normally performs the service. The couple stand on a platform called a **purowa**.

The couple usually give each other rings, and the thumbs on their right hands are sometimes tied together. Their right wrists may be tied together instead.

Children read special parts of the Buddhist Scriptures. The couple promise to love and respect each other. Sometimes there is a talk by a monk about Buddha's teaching on marriage, or the couple may go to the monastery after the ceremony.

Death

The friends and relations of a person who has died are sad because someone they love is not with them anymore. But Buddhists think that someone who has died will be reborn, so death is not the end. The funeral may be led by a monk who talks about the Buddha's teaching on what happens after death.

A Buddhist wedding in Malaysia

Buddhist monks at a funeral ceremony

Everyone repeats the Five Precepts and the Three Jewels, the most important things that Buddhists believe. The body of a Buddhist who has died is usually cremated.

Merit

Merit is the idea that doing something good can help you on your way to Nirvana. When someone dies, their relations often give presents to a monastery. They ask that the merit they gain from this should be shared with the person who has died.

They believe that this will help the person. For the same reason, every year at Buddhist festivals there are ceremonies to 'pass on' merit to people who have died. Buddhists think that performing these ceremonies can help people in their future lives.

New word

purowa special platform used in a marriage ceremony

Index